YOUR FLORIDA DIVORCE:

WORKING WITH THE LAW AND YOUR LAWYER

Tann H. Hunt
Attorney at Law

for

Kelly
Kathy
Karen

ISBN 0-931769-12-4

Library of Congress Catalog Card Number: 84-82509

EQUITY PRESS
P. O. Box 3841
Tallahassee, Florida 32315-3841

Printed in the United States of America.

Table of Contents

Introduction 5

Sex and the Single Pronoun 8

The One Hard and Fast Rule 10

Your Attorney 12

- Selection of an Attorney 12
- Attorney's Fees 14
- The Truth, the Whole Truth, and Nothing But the Truth 16
- Is Divorce the Right Thing to Do? 17

A Peek Under the Legal Tent, or More Than You May Want to Know About Our System of Law 18

Definitions 20

Simplified Dissolution of Marriage 40

Your Federal Taxes 44

The Divorce Itself 47

Your Appearance and Behavior 51

Alimony and Its Relatives 54

- Rehabilitative 57
- Permanent Periodic 57
- Lump Sum 59
- Equitable Distribution 61
- Special Equity 62
- The Marital Home 63
- The Two A's: Alimony and Adultery 64

The Children 67

Custody: New Shape, New Name 67
The Legislature's Dream World 69
The Real World 69
The New Tough Question 71
Grandparents 75
Fault Revisited 75
Who Goes Where? 76
Spouse Abuse 79
How is a Custody Decision Made? 80
Child Support 82
Support Versus Visitation 84
Modification 85
The Collection of Alimony and Child Support 87
Parental Conduct 88

The Future 89

Not to Worry—Forewarned is Forearmed—and Other Cliches 92

Appendix 93

A Simple Sample Petition for a Dissolution of Marriage 93
Affidavit for Custody of Children as Required by the Uniform Child Custody Jurisdiction Act 97
Worksheet for Preparing a Financial Affidavit 99
Financial Affidavit 106
Recommended Reading 111

Introduction

Maybe you've definitely decided to get a divorce—you've had it! Or maybe the idea is just one which stays in the back of your mind, coming out front and center only during a big fight. Or maybe you have no choice—your spouse is divorcing you. Or maybe you have a friend or relative involved in the divorce process and you wonder just what is back of the legal terms you're starting to hear. Regardless of which group you're in—or if you're just a curious soul who likes to read something different—this book will explain much of Florida divorce law and those related matters of property division and child custody.

This is not, repeat NOT, written as a "do-it-yourself" guide. Rightly or wrongly in the overall scheme of justice, most divorces should be handled by an attorney. It's worth noting that bright attorneys don't handle their own divorces. They hire another attorney.

This is, instead, a layman's guide to Florida divorce law—also called family law or domestic relations law. It is written in the hope that it will help you to understand the often confusing legal terms and practices. Should you become involved in a divorce, it will make working with the attorney easier and, maybe, even, less expensive. You don't have to pay a lawyer for the time you spend learning from this book.

While not written as a counseling/therapy book, it is written by an attorney who was divorced and who knows from personal experience that out of the frustration and disappointment can come a new and rewarding life.

Whether to go for counseling or not is a difficult decision for many people. They ask, "How can I get a good therapist? How can I pay for it?" The answers to those questions are almost as varied as the people asking the questions, but a few guidelines are available:

1. People you know who've been to counseling can give you opinions. But a counselor good for one person is not necessarily good for another. However, a friend's recommendation is a starting place. What matters is that you have a therapist you trust. Trial and error may be the only way to find the right one for you.
2. Your community Mental Health Association may be able to provide the service you need—or at least give you names from which to pick.

3. Often community mental health groups and church-based groups charge by a person's ability to pay.

Should you just not have the money or the temperament, some real help can be found on the printed page. At the end of this book is a list of books that other attorneys and I have found helpful to our clients.

Sex and the Single Pronoun

There's been a stir over the last few years about the sexual inequities in the English language, especially the pronoun system and how it is commonly applied. Those who wish the language they use to be more accurate, to reflect that positions and professions are occupied by members of both sexes, end up with what I consider to be awkward constructions or printings. "She/he," "(s)he," "his/her," and excessive use of "they/them," when a singular form would be more natural, are all clumsy.

Those who really care about the real inequities in our social system argue passionately that to do anything except "she/he," etc., reinforces the restricting belief that positions of power are held only by men—the dominant and dominating "he" and "his." Maybe. I don't really believe it. I believe the readers of this book are clever enough to look around them and see that more and more women are lawyers and that more than one or two are judges. The readers will also notice that more women are in law school than ever before.

Still, most attorneys in private practice are men. Most judges are men. Therefore, for this book, the lawyer and a judge will be "he."

For the purposes of this book, the client will, except for special subjects, be female and her spouse then will be "he."

Quoting a Delaware chancery judge, speaking of the lawyers who argue before him: "They're all gentlemen, except the ladies. I guess the ladies are gentlemen, too." So be it.

The One Hard and Fast Rule

Very little in this, as in any book about the law, can be written as a hard and fast rule. But there is one *Rule* that is hard and fast: Get your own lawyer. Do not share one with your spouse.

People ignore this Rule for two reasons: One, they really wish to save money, and they think this is a good way to do it. Two, they are so beaten down by the whole unhappiness of the marriage/divorce situation that they can't imagine that they have any rights worth hiring a lawyer to protect.

Saving money is great. But two people using the same lawyer is *not* the way to do it. Instead, brown-bag it for lunch every day. Skip lunch. Quit smoking. Quit drinking. Give up anything except your children's food and clothes before you give up your lawyer. The person who shares a lawyer with a spouse breathes new life into the cliche "penny wise, pound foolish." Lawyers are expensive, but a lop-sided agreement or a final judgment issued by a judge ignorant of your side will be even more expensive.

For those who feel "What's the use?" let me assure you that there *is* a tomorrow and a next month and a next year. Your feelings will change. What a lawyer should provide you is the chance to enjoy that future and not feel cheated. For those of you with children, never mind how *you* feel. You are responsible for those children and seeing that they are protected. You need a lawyer for them, if not for yourself.

Your Attorney

Selection of an Attorney

A difficult matter at best. If it helps any, it is just as difficult for a lawyer to pick a doctor or mechanic as it is for you to pick a lawyer.

One way: let your fingers do the walking. A trip through the Yellow Pages reveals that lawyers divide themselves up into areas of practice. The immigration specialist is not for you. Instead, search among the Family Law and General Practice names.

Calls to the offices of the attorneys should give you a general view of prices and the possibility of an initial half-hour conference, at a low rate, to let you get a sense of the person who may represent you.

Another way: check with family and friends who've recently been divorced. Ask them to tell you about the attorney in as much detail as you both can bear. Then have a "screening" interview with the one that sounds best to you. Remember that what is best for a friend may not be best for you. A father/mother figure may be what your psyche needs, but then again you may be happier with a more clipped, no-nonsense type.

It is sometimes suggested that you call the Florida Bar and have it make a recommendation from its Lawyer Referral Service. This is not a bad idea as long as you know just what the referral means.

Lawyers place their names with the Florida Bar Lawyer Referral Service. To do so, all they have to do is be members of the Florida Bar (one must be a member to practice law in Florida at all) and swear that they have professional liability insurance (malpractice insurance). They also agree to charge only ten dollars for the initial half-hour consultation. Some lawyers also agree to charge reduced rates for the poor or elderly. Lawyers tell the Referral Service which legal areas they wish referrals to be in and which they don't want—divorces, but not securities; real estate but not criminal, for example. That's it. The rest is just a matter of rotation.

If, when you call, Lawyer D is at the top of the list, that's the name you get. If you'd waited and called the next day, it might have been Lawyer Q at the top of the list. In other words, the Bar merely gives you the name at the top in both your legal and geographic area. The Bar does not promise that the lawyer is especially skilled, experienced or sympathetic—only that the lawyer is a member of the

Bar, insured, and one who wants cases in your area.

Attorney's Fees

Talk fees with the lawyer(s) you consult. Legal fees, like cars, can be paid for on time. Be honest about your finances. Pay what you say you will and do it when you say you will. Treat a lawyer fairly and he will be willing to work with you on fees.

Your lawyer will know that if your well-off husband has left you with barely enough money to buy food for your children, you still may be able to pay a lawyer to get you a divorce and a fair property settlement. The judge may order the husband to pay your attorney's fees and other court costs even though that money is used to oppose your husband. And if the judge orders him to pay child support and, later, he fails to do so, his impoverished wife can bring him back to court expecting that the delinquent husband will again be assessed the court costs and her attorney's fees.

Florida law, as written in the Florida Statutes, tells us:

> §61.16 Attorney's fees, suit money, and costs. The court may from time to time,

> after considering the financial resources of both parties, order a party to pay a reasonable amount for attorney's fees, suit money, and the cost to the other party of maintaining or defending any proceeding under this chapter, including enforcement and modification proceedings. The court may order that the amount be paid directly to the attorney, who may enforce the order in his name.

The Florida Legislature has given us this statute out of a very clear sense of "fair's fair." Both parties, not just the well-off husband, will be able to hire competent legal help. *Cummings v. Cummings*, 330 So.2d 134 (Fla. 1976). To insure that the equitable distribution of property is not undone by the less affluent spouse having to pay fees, a court ordered award is appropriate. *Mahaffey v. Mahaffey*, 401 So.2d 1372 (Fla. 5th DCA 1981). What the names and numbers mean is explained under *case law* in the "Definitions" section.

As with alimony and child support, fees are awarded on the basis of the asking party's need and the other party's ability to pay.

Should you have no money—nothing—then you should consult the Florida Bar as to how to get in touch with Legal Services or Legal Aid in your community. These agencies may be able to help you if your income level is low enough and their budget high enough.

The Truth, The Whole Truth and Nothing But the Truth

That's what you should tell your lawyer. This is especially important if *any* elements of your divorce proceedings have a chance of being contested.

While adultery and any other misconduct have nothing to do with the granting of the dissolution (that's no-fault) they may have a great effect on property division, alimony, and custody. Your lawyer cannot help you if he doesn't have all the relevant information—and your lawyer is a better judge of what is relevant than you are.

Remember—your relationship with your lawyer is confidential. What you tell him is secret—at least it is secret in that he will not tell anyone—without your consent. The danger to you from not telling your lawyer something which you are ashamed or uncomfortable about is that it may not be a secret from your spouse, his witnesses, and *his* lawyer.

Your lawyer cannot help you if the first news of your affair or drinking problem comes to him at the hearing.

Is Divorce "The Right Thing to Do"?

This is *not* a question your attorney can answer for you. However, your attorney can give you information to use in making a decision. From your attorney should come an analysis of your legal and financial situation. Your attorney should be able to make an educated prediction, *not a promise*, as to how a judge will rule on your case. Armed with these pieces of information you will be better equipped to reach a decision on your own. And that's whose decision it should be—not your mother's, not your clergyman's, not your neighbor's. While advice from them may be comforting and helpful, the final decision is yours alone.

Once you do decide to seek a divorce, once you have selected an attorney whom you trust, get your legal advice only from this attorney. This is not the time to listen to your sister talk about her neighbor who got the house, the car, the kids and $1,500 a month.

A Peek Under the Legal Tent, or More Than You May Want to Know About our System of Law

Law comes in two forms. One form is the Florida Statutes as written by the Florida Legislature. A sample passage was quoted in a previous section. These statutes are what the average person is referring to when he asks, "What does the law say?" That question can be answered by reading the relevant statute. Or so it seems.

But—it is not that simple. What the law "says" is determined by what judges say the law says. The judges' saying of "what the law says" is what we call case law. In other words, when there is a dispute as to what the law says about a particular situation, there is a "case" which goes to Court. In Florida, divorces are heard by a circuit judge. After a hearing of the evidence and the application of statute law and, perhaps, case law, the judge reaches a decision. This decision, by itself, is not case law. However, if one of the parties feels wronged by the decision—and if he has the money to pursue the matter—he appeals to a higher court. This higher court hears, not the evidence again, but rather the arguments of the attorneys as to the correctness of the circuit judge's decision. The decision of this higher court, a district court of appeals in Florida, is then the case law. These higher court decisions are printed up and made available to all.

Thus, when another case goes to trial the attorneys can point to (can cite) the case law written by the appeals court and can argue that it applies to (controls) the situation before the trial court now.

Once the appeals court has reached its decision, the party which now feels wronged might be able to appeal to the Florida Supreme Court. Until recently, all it took to appeal to the Supreme Court was determination and money. Now—since 1980—one must also have a case which falls into a particular class of cases.

Bluntly, one's chance of getting a divorce case all the way up to the Supreme Court is small.

Definitions

Some of the following definitions you will find complete within themselves. Others will not be really clear until you've read on into the chapters dealing with those subjects. Still others may never be really clear to you. Don't feel bad. Great legal minds are not in full agreement as to their meaning.

Divorce. Legally, there is no such thing in Florida. There hasn't been since 1971 when the state legislature in its linguistic wisdom changed "divorce" to "dissolution of marriage." For the purposes of this book, the two terms will be used interchangeably.

No-fault. The type of divorce law we have had in Florida since 1971. Before 1971, a person seeking to shed her spouse had to complain of some pretty sordid behavior before she could get out of an unhappy marriage. Now all the shedding spouse must do is allege that the marriage is "irretrievably broken." Gone are the semi-public airings of charges of adultery or cruelty. Well, almost gone. While these charges have no place in the action for divorce, they may appear in a property or custody fight, more often the custody fight. More on this later.

Service of Process. The presentation to your spouse of your petition for dissolution and your summons. This must be done, for a fee, by a sheriff's deputy or someone appointed by the sheriff to deliver such papers. The server then returns to the petitioner's lawyer a "return of service" which reports where and when the service was made. The *when* is especially important should the served spouse not respond and the petitioner wishes a default to be entered. The twenty-day period after which a default can be entered starts with the service. This is not something you can do yourself; for the point of the law on the subject is to insure that it be done by an impartial person who can swear that it was done—that your spouse did receive notice of your pending legal action and, thereby, has the chance to respond, to defend himself. While obviously it would be cheaper if you could just do it yourself, you have to concede that some people would lie and say there had been service when there had not been.

Variations on the requirement of personal service

are allowed in some situations. Your attorney will know what is appropriate if the standard method is not possible.

Jurisdiction: Part I. Florida has a multi-layered court system: county court, circuit court, district appeals court, and the Supreme Court. It is the circuit court which has jurisdiction over divorce cases on the trial level. Once the circuit court judge has ruled, a dissatisfied former spouse may take the case to the district court of appeals. Those dissatisfied after that process may, under limited conditions, the full explaining of which is beyond the scope of this book, take the case to the Florida Supreme Court. The next part of jurisdiction is the question as to whether or not a person comes under the jurisdiction of the court.

Jurisdiction: Part II. Another meaning of jurisdiction is a court's authority to hear a case and to direct the behavior of the parties as a result of its decision in that case. The court gets this jurisdiction, not through anything it does, but rather through the behavior of the spouse filing the petition for divorce. To create jurisdiction, the petitioner must have been a resident of Florida for six months *before* filing for divorce.

> Florida Statutes 61.021 Residence required. To obtain a dissolution of marriage the party filing the proceeding must reside 6 months in the state before filing the petition, but this does not affect any suit filed before October 1, 1957.

Usually proof of residency is obtained by the petitioning spouse swearing at the hearing that she has been a resident for the proper time and by having a witness swear that he knows from personal observation that the spouse was a resident of Florida for six months before filing for divorce.

Sometimes, the question of what is *residency* arises. To be a resident one must actually physically be in the state and have the intent to be a resident. "Actually, physically in the state" does not mean that one couldn't have been gone on a business trip or a vacation.

Should the matter be contested, your lawyer will know how to prove, in detail, your residency. Should you want to leave the state after filing, please check with your attorney.

Petitioner. In its attempt to remove the divorce procedure from the win/lose atmosphere of the regular civil courtroom, the legislature decided that the person filing for the divorce, the one making the allegation that the marriage is over and the one asking the court to order certain actions about property and children, would be called the Petitioner rather than the Plaintiff, the term used in a regular civil suit.

Petition. This is what the Petitioner files. A sample is in the Appendix.

Respondent. The legislature decided that the person whom the Petitioner sued for divorce would be the Respondent and not the Defendant. This does sound a bit better when one thinks that the accused in a criminal case is also the Defendant.

Answer. This is the response made by one spouse when the other initiates a petition for dissolution of the marriage. In it the answering spouse agrees or disagrees with the statements (allegations) made in the petition. If the divorce is a "friendly" one, now is the time to tell the judge that an agreement as to child custody, support, alimony, and property has been worked out. This agreement does not have to be accepted by the judge, but it may be.

Counterpetition. This is what the respondent can file in addition to an answer. It sets out what the respondent wants from the dissolution. There are certain financial and tactical advantages to filing a counterpetition and your attorney can explain these to you.

Default. This is the name used for those cases in which (1) the personally served spouse does nothing; (2) twenty days from personal service of process pass; and (3) then the clerk of the court enters a default. The court may then enter a judgment granting the dissolution, and may order alimony and child support. Child custody, too, can be decided when the spouse is in default. For "good cause," a default can be set aside. The Court decides what is good cause.

Hearing. The time when your case is heard by the judge. If it were not a family law matter it would be called a trial. Some people and some laws use the words interchangeably.

Financial Affidavit. If you want a judge to order alimony, child support, or attorney's fees, you must prepare a financial affidavit for both the judge and the other side.

The affidavit, which you must swear is the truth, can be very useful to you and your attorney. Most of us, even those of us who are careful with money and live within our means, don't know *where* the money goes. Unless we keep penny-by-penny records, we have no idea how much is spent on school supplies, snacks, non-prescription medical stuff the kids need—and so on. Keep that penny-by-penny record and you will be in a good position to defend what you're asking for child support as opposed to alimony. Remember, children get haircuts, too, and use shampoo—all at a price. Detailed recordkeeping helps your lawyer help you and often impresses a judge.

The law requiring the financial affidavit doesn't come from statute law. It comes, instead, from the Rules of Civil Procedure as adopted by the Florida Supreme Court.

> Rule 1.611 Dissolution of Marriage (Divorce)
>
> a) Financial Statement. Every application for temporary alimony, child support, attorneys' fees or suit money shall be accompanied by an affidavit specifying the party's financial circumstances. The affidavit shall be served at the same time that notice of hearing on the application is served. The opposing party shall make an affidavit about his financial circumstances and shall serve it before or at the hearing. If no application for a temporary award is

> made, the parties shall make and serve the affidavits at least 10 days before the trial if permanent alimony, child support, attorneys' fees or suit money is sought. If a party is not represented by an attorney, sufficient time will be allowed the party to prepare the required affidavit at hearing or trial.

A copy of a financial affidavit form is included in the back of this book.

Case Law. This, in contrast to statute law written by the Legislature, is written by the judges as they apply the statute law to specific cases. What the circuit judge who actually hears the parties in divorce hearing decides is not what we call case law. We don't get case law until at least one party is dissatisfied with the rulings or judgment by the circuit judge and appeals to the appellate court, the district court of appeals. What this court decides is case law—unless and until the Supreme Court overrules that appellate court. The Supreme Court opinion is, then, the case law on that specific point of statute law.

To use the best known case in alimony/divorce law as an example: The trial court gave Mrs. Canakaris lump sum alimony of $50,000, her husband's interest in their jointly owned house, $500 per week permanent periodic alimony, and half of the real estate they owned as tenants by the entirety. Dr. Canakaris appealed to the First District Court of Appeal claiming that this was too much for him to pay and that the trial court, under previous case law, had no right to give his wife his part of the house nor so much periodic alimony. The First District Court agreed with Dr. Canakaris and its opinion became case law printed for all the world to see in the Southern Reporter, Second Series as *Canakaris v. Canakaris*, 356 So.2d 858 (Fla. 1st DCA 1978).

The 356 is the volume number. So.2d means Southern Reporter, Second Series. 858 is the page number. (Fla. 1st DCA 1978) tells you that it was a Florida case in the First District Court of Appeal in 1978. The Southern Reporter also prints the opinions of courts in Alabama, Mississippi, and Louisiana.

That would have been that, but Mrs. Canakaris thought the 1st DCA was wrong and she had the funds to follow up. She went to the Florida Supreme Court which said in an opinion which we'll look at much more closely in the section on alimony, "Mrs. Canakaris, you're right. Dr. Canakaris, give her the $500 per week and your half of the house." So we have new case law: *Canakaris v. Canakaris*, 382

So.2d 1197 (Fla. 1980). Cases which are widely known and discussed are referred to by just one name—rather like using a friend's first name only. Thus, this repeatedly written and talked about case is called simply *Canakaris*. In divorces one doesn't have to decide which side of the *v.* to use. The big problem with *Canakaris* is how to pronounce it.

Dependent Children. Children are legally dependent up to age eighteen. At that point, no matter how foolish acting, they are legally adults, able to vote, and we *real* adults are no longer required to support them whether we are married or divorced.

Sad exception: Should one of our children be mentally or physically handicapped and unable to be self-supporting, that child remains dependent on us until he is able to be self-supporting. This can be at age thirty-five or never.

Judge. A judge is a lawyer who has had at least five years practice as an attorney in Florida and who has been elected to the position by his fellow citizens in his judicial circuit. To hear divorce cases, one must be a circuit judge as opposed to a county judge; one is elected for six years. To be a judge one need not have any special experience or training. Once elected, one is sent to various judges' schools and conferences.

Those who hear and decide cases at the appellate level are also called judges; those who labor at the Supreme Court level are called justices.

A judge, alas, has no special blessing from God, no granting of Solomon-like wisdom. Judges are, within the legal framework, ordinary people. Some are religious, some not. Some happily married, some unhappily married, some divorced. Some have children of whom they are proud, about whose raising they are pleased. Some have children who bring disgrace and worry, creating guilt and blaming. All these factors and others can influence a judge and enter into his perception of the facts placed before him.

In the deciding of the matters before them in family law cases, judges have great discretion, which is respected by the appeals courts. If reasonable men can differ, the trial court's decision is not overturned. "It is not the function of the Appellate Court to substitute its judgment for that of the Trial Court through reevaluation of the testimony and evidence." *Kevin v. Kevin*, 442 So.2d 203 (Fla. 1983).

While one doesn't have to be special to be a circuit court judge, it may be true that something "special" happens to a person who becomes a judge. Not that he becomes all wise, all knowing, but rather that the awesome responsibility of the position forces him to be more reflective, more inclined to look at all aspects of the human dilemma placed before him. We can only hope this is so.

Venue. This means the county where the petition for dissolution is filed and heard. Dissolution statute law doesn't say anything about venue, so one must see what the laws about venue, in general, say.

> Florida Statute 47.011 Where actions may be begun. Actions shall be brought only in the county where the defendant resides, where the cause of action accrued, or where the property in litigation is located. This section shall not apply to actions against non-residents.

How this general statute law translates into case law can be found in a recent opinion from the First District Court of Appeal. The Court held that one county rather than another was where the intact marriage existed, where the respondent lives, where the litigated property was, and even where "the precipitating event for her seeking a divorce . . . and alleged assault" took place—and thus where venue should be. *Crawford v. Crawford*, 415 So.2d 870 (Fla. 1st DCA 1982).

Venue, however, can be waived (not made an issue) thereby allowing both parties to agree to have their divorce in a county where there is no newspaper interested in their fight.

Stipulations and Agreements. These words (meaning almost the same thing and often used together) describe what the parties themselves can work out. They then request that a court "order" the terms of the agreement by incorporating the agreement into the final judgment. Thus, you can have a detailed agreement of many pages and a one page final judgment.

An agreement written by the parties has many virtues over a judgment written by a judge. The parties can negotiate an agreement which neither of them is greatly pleased with but one which neither finds intolerable.

More than one judge argues strongly that the lawyers can reach a better balanced resolution than the judge can. According to the judges with this view, the lawyers, having lived with the case for months, know the clients and the facts better than the judge would be able to after a hearing which usually takes one to four hours. These lawyers, acting in good faith, can create, and urge their clients to accept, an agreement which is both fair and responsive to the clients' special needs.

The fairness of such an agreement is only as great as the good will of the parties and the skill of the lawyers allows. A strong-willed spouse, with or without a lawyer, can run over a weak-willed spouse who either doesn't have a lawyer or who has told the lawyer that he or she (usually she) doesn't want to try for a better deal.

Despite the advice of their attorneys, some spouses sign agreements which are, to the objective eye, greatly against the signer's best interest. An attorney in such a situation may have the client also sign a statement saying that the client knew she was acting against her attorney's advice. This protects the attorney from later claims of malpractice and should impress on the client just how awful the attorney thinks the agreement is.

A word of caution: Generally, it is harder to modify the custody, visitation, support or alimony provisions of a final judgment which incorporates an agreement reached by the parties than one which a judge orders after hearing both sides. Check with your lawyer about this point, especially for child support and alimony amounts.

Discovery. This could be called the lawyer's homework. It is the rather dull, non-dramatic, non-

Perry Mason way of finding out information about the client's spouse, his fitness as a parent and his financial condition. There are six methods by which discovery can be made. They are the following:

1. Financial Affidavits: These are *required* by law if permanent alimony, child support, attorneys' fees or suit money are at issue. Notice that *both* parties must file affidavits. An affidavit is a sworn statement. A sample is in the back of the book.
2. Depositions: These take place *before* the hearing. They are the taking of sworn testimony, in response to questions, in order for the attorney taking the deposition to learn the other side of the case. Thus, the lawyer is better prepared to plan and present the client's case at the hearing or to draw up a settlement which is as favorable as possible to the client. Depositions may be taken from both parties and from prospective witnesses.
3. Interrogatories: This is a fancy word for written questions which must be answered under oath. Often these ask that the person answering the question attach documents such as income tax returns. This is a way of saving some time and money by getting documents this way rather than by Requests to Produce.

4. Requests to Produce: This is a formal way of asking for documents, photographs, and other tangible things. Often it is combined with the notice setting the time of the deposition. Requests for Production are also used to get records from people such as employers, whose depositions need not be taken.
5. Requests for Admissions: These really are not used to discover information, but rather to get the other side to admit the truth of an alleged fact or the genuineness of a document. They, therefore, are highly useful as a way to limit the issues which must be argued at the hearing.
6. Motions for Physical and Mental Examinations: Notice that these are motions only. In other words, only the Court can order the physical or mental examination and only for good cause. The judge decides what is good cause. As a rule, these motions are used when the fitness of a parent is at issue. A motion is a request to the Court; the Court must formally grant it or nothing happens.

Uniform Child Custody Jurisdiction Act Affidavit. If you are filing a petition for divorce and have minor children, you must comply with the requirements of the Uniform Child Custody Jurisdiction Act. You must, in a sworn statement, tell the court the names and ages of your children. You must tell the court the addresses of the children for the last five years and with whom they have lived during this time. You must tell the court if the children are involved in any other litigation. A sample affidavit is in the Appendix.

The purpose portion of the Florida law speaks for itself and is supported by what we've all recently seen on TV—the anguish of a parent whose child was snatched.

> Florida Statute 61.1304 Purposes of act; construction of provisions.—The general purposes of this act are to:
>
> 1. Avoid jurisdictional competition and conflict with courts of other states in matters of child custody which have in the past resulted in the shifting of children from state to state with harmful effects on their well-being.
>
> 2. Promote cooperation with the courts of other states to the end that a custody decree is rendered in the state which can best decide the case in the interest of the child.
>
> 3. Assure that litigation concerning the custody of a child takes place ordinarily in the state with which the child and his family have the closest connection and where

significant evidence concerning his care, protection, training, and personal relationships is most readily available, and that courts of this state decline the exercise of jurisdiction when the child and his family have a closer connection with another state.

4. Discourage continuing controversies over child custody in the interest of the greater stability of home environment and of secure family relationships for the child.

5. Deter abductions and other unilateral removals of children undertaken to obtain custody awards.

6. Avoid relitigation of custody decisions of other states in this state insofar as feasible.

7. Facilitate the enforcement of custody decrees of other states.

8. Promote and expand the exchange of information and other forms of mutual assistance between the courts of this state and those of other states concerned with the same child.

9. Make uniform the law with respect to the subject of this act among states enacting it.

Some parents avoid the whole subject of child custody jurisdiction law by just snatching the child and making a run for it. For those of you so tempted, consider:

1. It's wrong—against the law. What example are you setting for your child?
2. You are creating a world of grief and confusion for your child. By wiping out the child's past with a new name and history, you distort the future.
3. When caught—and the odds for your being caught increase each day—your moral and legal position before a judge is almost zero. Unless the parent from whom you snatched the child was a proven child abuser, your chances of having other than supervised visitation are minute. If the other parent *is* a child abuser then that's what Child Protective Services and the courts are for.

Property. This means what you own. It comes in two types which are important in divorce cases: *personal* and *real*. In the world of law, *real* property means land, real estate. In contrast, *personal* property is everything else—the diamonds, the pearls, the Chinese art collection. Some interesting fights have come about over whether the washing machine was part of the house (a fixture) and, thus, part of real property, or separate and, thus, personal property.

Vest. Not one part of a three piece suit. In the language of law, the word is used to describe the state or process of a right, usually a money right, belonging to some one as in "His pension rights vest after ten years." For our purposes, an example is "child support vests in the child, rather than in the mother." So, while the child support is paid to the mother, she can't give away the child's right by saying to the father, "Just go away. Don't bother us again. Don't even send money."

Adultery. A sexual relationship outside of marriage after the marriage has been made and not—yet?—broken. It is an *extra*marital affair compared to a *pre*marital affair. Under Florida law, the sexual relationship does not have to be heterosexual. A homosexual extra-marital affair is also adultery. *Patin v. Patin*, 371 So.2d 682 (Fla. 4th DCA 1979). In colonial America a woman who committed anything even close to adultery—pre-extra-post—was punished by her community and frequently was forced to wear a scarlet letter A on the front of her dress. The expressions "scarlet women" or "scarlet-lettered women" still live in our language revealing that we are still a long way from social/sexual equality. The term is never used for adulterous men.

Simplified Dissolution of Marriage

In June, 1984, some new Florida legal rules regarding divorce came into being. They have been in effect too short a time for anyone to say how well they will work.

The object of these rules is to make it easier for those without dependent children to get a divorce on the cheap without having to pay for a lawyer.

For people who have been married for only six awful months and who own jointly only a waterbed and a stereo, this change in the rules will be the blessing their marriage vows weren't. For those who have been married twenty-two years, whose kids are grown, who own a house and other property—real or personal—the new rules contain real risks.

The risks are those that spring from ignorance, fear and stress. In other words, one spouse may, by sheer brute force of spirit and will, get the other spouse to agree to a simple non-lawyer divorce on the terms the bully wants. Note: not all bullies are men.

Certain conditions must be met for a couple to use the simple rules:

1. There must be no children under 18 or dependent children.
2. The wife is not pregnant.
3. One spouse has lived in Florida for the last six months.

Once these conditions are satisfied, the couple qualifies to use the new rules. They then get from the clerk of the circuit court in their county the twenty-two page booklet prepared by the Florida Bar with the approval of the Florida Supreme Court. Remarkably well-written, the booklet and its forms can be studied at home. However, the petition for dissolution of marriage has to be signed in front of a clerk of the court, and by both spouses. In addition, the couple must provide the clerk with something called a certificate of corroborating witness. This certificate corroborates that one spouse or the other has lived in Florida for the six months immediately preceding the signing of the petition. This certificate must be signed by someone who knows about that period of residence from his own experience, and it must be signed in the presence of some notary public, or in the presence of the clerk of the court, at the time the petition for dissolution of marriage is signed.

And that, ladies and gentlemen, is that. The booklet recommends that the husband and wife fill out the financial affidavits, copies of which are in the booklet, and recommends that the couple fill out the property settlement, also included in the booklet. However, the rules are such that the financial affidavits and property settlement forms can be ignored. This way—for those beyond the waterbed/stereo stage of marriage—lies disaster.

At this writing, the judge's role in all this is still not entirely clear. But weight of precedent (legalese for what's happened before) tells us that he cannot act as an attorney for one party or the other, trying to determine if the agreement is fair. All he can do is see that the required papers are in order. Time, of course, will tell if the judges will feel compelled to be more active in the face of possible spouse bullying—or of blatant unfairness. Appeals are not allowed under this simplified procedure.

Time, of course, will also tell us if this change in the rules was a good idea or not. Legal analysis will tell us how many cases return to the courts with one party yelling, "I've been robbed and the rules helped the robbing take place." Social analysis will tell us how many couples are now singles saying, "Gee, it was great and look at the bucks we saved."

Your Federal Taxes

When your spirits are at their lowest, when you feel no one cares about your suffering and your divorce, take heart. Someone does care. Many collective someones—the Internal Revenue Service.

As you change your married status, so do you change your tax status. Maybe for the better, maybe for the worse. Some tax changes you will have little or no control over. Others, with the help of a tax smart lawyer, you can control to your benefit. Not all lawyers are tax smart. Those who aren't don't need to be if they are tax aware. They send their clients to a CPA and work with that professional's advice to structure the best divorce/tax deal possible for the client.

The following are a few tax certainties for you to be aware of now. For the fine points of these and for the fancy footwork of dancing to the IRS's tune, consult your attorney.

Alimony is a deduction for the person paying it and taxable income to the person receiving it. Child support—no matter how much—is not deductible, nor is it taxable income to the person receiving it. Already you can see some bargaining points if the amounts are high enough. Warning: Unless the final judgment spells out exactly what payments are for, all the money will be counted by IRS as alimony. More bargaining is possible as to the form the alimony takes—lump sum, periodic, mortgage payments, taxes, insurance.

Who get the child(ren) as a tax deduction is a tricky and important question, for it has an effect on the child care deduction and the medical deductions. Generally, the child deduction goes to the parent with custody or whose home is the primary residence for the child(ren) in a shared parental responsibility situation. With that deduction comes the possibility of another tax blessing: the head of household deduction. There are fine points to these general observations which your lawyer can apply for your benefit if your case fits one of the many nooks and crannies of the tax code.

The Federal 1984 tax laws made major changes about property transferred from one spouse to another. These changes were intended to simplify divorce law and reduce the role of the federal government in divorce actions. The reactions of the tax experts in the American Bar Association is that the laws produced just the opposite result. These experts are now lobbying Congress for further change. The new law has one "virtue." It appears evenhanded in its sexual bias: the property transfer laws tend to favor the husband; the alimony laws tend to favor the wife, if the alimony is short term. *PROCEED WITH CAUTION.*

The Divorce Itself

The introduction of the term "the marriage is irretrievably broken" came with the "no-fault" concept of divorce. No longer do you have to expose your life by telling the judge that your husband beats you, drinks to excess, gambles all on the dogs. Just say, under oath, "The marriage is irretrievably broken." Some judges want a bit more. For such a judge (your lawyer will know if your case is assigned to one), some general, yet honest, statement about non-communication should do it.

> Florida Statute 61.052 (2) Based on the evidence at the hearing, which evidence need not be corroborated except to establish that the residence requirements of s. 61.021 are met, the court shall dispose of the petition for dissolution of marriage as follows, when the petition is based on the allegation that the marriage is irretrievably broken:

The corroboration of the residency requirements

is usually accomplished by the petitioner's having a friend testify under oath that the petitioner has been a resident of Florida for the six months before the petition was filed.

> Florida Statute 61.052 (2)(a) If there are no minor children of the marriage and if the respondent does not, by answer to the petition for dissolution, deny that the marriage is irretrievably broken, the court shall enter a judgment of dissolution of the marriage if the court finds that the marriage is irretrievably broken.

Under these conditions, with the petitioner swearing the marriage is over, it would take some very unusual circumstances for the judge to not find the marriage irretrievably broken. However:

> Florida Statute 61.052 (2)(b) When there are minor children of the marriage or when the respondent denies by answer to the petition for dissolution that the marriage is irretrievably broken, the court may:
>
> 1. Order either or both parties to consult with a marriage counselor, psychologist, psychiatrist, minister, priest, rabbi, or any other person deemed qualified by the court and acceptable to the party or parties ordered to seek consultation; or

2. Continue the proceedings for a reasonable length of time not to exceed 3 months, to enable the parties themselves to effect a reconciliation; or,

3. Take such other action as may be in the best interest of the parties and the minor children of the marriage.

There is no question that the court has power to order consultation with a marriage counselor, etc. There is, however, a real question of the value of any counseling to which a person is *ordered.* There is, more likely, value in the up to three months cooling off period. We have—alas—no figures to show if this judicial activism saves marriages. The value, though, might not be in "saved" marriages but in divorces which are turned from hateful to tolerable.

Florida Statute 61.052
If at any time, the court finds that the marriage is irretrievably broken, the court shall enter a judgement of dissolution of the marriage. If the court finds that the marriage is not irretrievably broken, it shall deny the petition for dissolution of marriage.

(3) During any period of continuance the court may make appropriate orders for the support and alimony of the parties; the custody, support, maintenance and educa-

> tion of the minor children of the marriage; attorney's fees; and the preservation of the property of the parties.

This means that while you are waiting through a court ordered continuance, the court can protect you and your property. The same protection is available to a spouse and children who are waiting to get a final hearing on a crowded court docket. The court can hold a hearing on temporary custody, support, and alimony while discovery goes on to gather information for a final hearing.

> (4) A judgment of dissolution of marriage shall result in each spouse having the status of being single and unmarried. No judgment of dissolution of marriage renders the children of such marriage illegitimate.

Your Appearance and Behavior

How you appear to the judge does make a difference. Years of being told "Don't judge a book by its cover" haven't made any more of an impression on the judge than they have on you. The way people dress and their manner during the hearing do influence the judge.

Some judges are reluctant to admit how much they are influenced by appearance. However, Judge Carl H. Harper in West Palm Beach, in his opinion in the much reported, lengthy Pulitzer trial, gave us an insight into judicial reactions which we rarely have in print:

> At this time, the court feels it appropriate to comment on the demeanor of the parties as it relates to their credibility and in weighing the evidence. Although the court was busily engaged in taking detailed, copious notes during the lengthy trial, the court nevertheless closely observed the ap-

> pearance and demeanor of the witnesses, and in particular the parties, through the trial. As to the husband, this court could readily observe the embarrassment, painful hurt and frustrating concern exuding from his doleful eyes and aging face. By contrast, the wife sat at the table "doodling" on a note pad as though unconcerned. As the husband and his witness, Janice Nelson, were testifying, the wife engaged them in vitriolic stares, eventually staring them down. Frankly, the court was somewhat relieved when, toward the end of the eighteen day trial, the wife finally broke into tears, necessitating a brief recess, indicating that she was, after all, capable of human emotion and concern. The husband's testimony and evidence had the ring of truth, whereas the denials of the wife and her paramours were patently false and knowingly given.

Additional note: Just as much care should be given to one's appearance and manner during a deposition as during the hearing itself. It is during the deposition that the opposing lawyer has a chance to size you up and evaluate how the judge will see you. If the opposing lawyer sees you as well-dressed and composed under stress, he will have a different view of the effect of your testimony than if you are sloppy and highly nervous.

What is "well-dressed"? Not disco fancy, not grocery store casual. "Well-dressed" is church or temple dress. Many gold chains are for Christmas trees or pawn shops, not custody hearings. Heavy make-up and multiple eyelashes may increase your social life; they will not increase your alimony payments. T-shirts and jackets with sayings of any sort—risqué or otherwise—are of dubious value anywhere. They have no value in a hearing room. "Good ole boy" denim outfits and billed caps don't convince a judge that the wearer works harder than one who knows enough to wear a regular shirt and jacket and take his hat off.

Alimony and its Relatives

Alimony, like much in family law, is changing. In the old days, for the middle and upper classes, alimony was what the husband paid his ex-wife—for the rest of his life or until her remarriage. Some called it the price of exiting.

Alimony rarely was a concern of those in the lower economic levels. If the husband had any funds over what was needed to keep himself alive, they went to child support. Once that was taken care of, there often wasn't enough left for the paying of alimony.

Now, alimony, for a variety of reasons, has undergone many changes of purposes and name. In many intact families, the wife and mother works full-time outside the home. In some families, this working is financially necessary to maintain what the couple requires for its standard of living. In others, the wife works to satisfy her sense of self, to use her education and abilities, or to escape the often boring routine of housework and child care.

This work outside the home, for whatever reason,

is proof that she can be employed and can pay for some, if not all, of her own needs and those of the children. Since the old rationale for alimony was that it supported a woman who could not support herself, the courts no longer find the same need for alimony that they once did.

This doesn't mean that alimony no longer exists; it means only that it has changed form and duration. Without being tiresome, it is worth remembering that in 1984 on the average a woman earned only 57 cents for every dollar a man earned. With this economic inequity before it, the court has to look at each case separately.

> Florida Statute 61.08 Alimony.
>
> 1. In a proceeding for dissolution of marriage, the court may grant alimony to either party, which alimony may be rehabilitative or permanent in nature. In any award of alimony, the court may order periodic payments or payments in lump sum or both. The court may consider the adultery of a spouse and the circumstances thereof in determining whether alimony shall be awarded to such spouse and the amount of alimony, if any, to be awarded.
>
> 2. In determining a proper award of alimony or maintenance, the court shall consider all relevant economic factors, including but not limited to:

a. The standard of living established during the marriage.

b. The duration of the marriage.

c. The age and the physical and emotional condition of both parties.

d. The financial resources of each party.

e. Where applicable, the time necessary for either party to acquire sufficient education or training to enable him or her to find appropriate employment.

f. The contribution of each party to the marriage, including, but not limited to, services rendered in homemaking, child care, education, and career building of the other party.

The court may consider any other factor necessary to do equity and justice between the parties.

Alimony can be paid by the husband to the wife or the wife to the husband. You will not be burdened with an explanation as to why the first is more common.

Alimony, if ordered by the court, can come in three forms. One person can receive any or all of these.

Rehabilitative

What one spouse pays to another in the hope that the receiving spouse will become self-supporting and thus not eligible for permanent periodic alimony. A judge orders this only if he is convinced that the receiving spouse can, through education or training, support herself at a level equal to that of the marriage. In other words, a doctor's wife of twenty years cannot be sent back to college to renew her teaching certificate after twenty years of not working outside the home. The doctor cannot walk away with paying only her tuition and expenses for a year. Also, if the spouse, despite a good faith effort, is not rehabilitated by the end of the rehab alimony period, the rehab alimony can be extended or converted to plain periodic permanent alimony.

Permanent Periodic

This means, for all practical purposes, monthly payments until one of the spouses dies or the receiving spouse remarries.

The assumption is that the receiving spouse has earned the right to be supported in the style of the marriage and should be so supported until death or remarriage. But cold economic reality offers the chance for alimony to relatively few. First, alimony of any type is seldom awarded except after many years of marriage. Your lawyer can tell you where your marriage/divorce fits in this scheme of things. Second, there can be no alimony without funds from which to pay it. All too often, a marriage of many years breaks up because of the husband's drinking and job failure. The wife is then lucky to get child support.

Or—again all too often—what was enough, just barely, to support a couple and their children is now only enough to support the husband and provide some child support payments. The wife, if not working before the divorce, will be after.

Alimony, in one sense, is like child support. The amount is determined by the need of the spouse requesting alimony and by the paying ability of the other spouse. Both these factors are judged by the standard of living of the parties during the marriage. A divorced wife can certainly live on $12,000; but if her husband earns $200,000 per year and they spent $12,000 a year just for one servant, the court will not consider $12,000 per year fair alimony.

In setting alimony, once the judge has looked at need and ability and standard of living, he then examines the length of the marriage, the rehabilitative potential of the alimony-seeking spouse, and what the alimony-seeking spouse did for the marriage. This last consideration is most interesting, for it allows the judge to do what he can't find himself able to do under any other label. The judge does look at homemaking/child care and the traditional wife's contribution to a husband's career— entertaining the spouse's business friends. For those wives who worked to put their husbands through professional school, here is where the court allows some payback. The Florida courts, unlike some elsewhere, do not consider a professional degree marital property with a specific dollar value which could be split as could be a house. However, Florida does let the courts do what needs to be done—make the husband repay the wife for the years spent in a dull, lowpaying job with little or no chance for her own career advancement.

Lump Sum

This is one of those legal terms that means almost exactly what it says: alimony paid in one lump sum. This form of alimony, if the only form ordered, has one virtue: assuming there are no dependent children, it lets the parties be done with each other. However, lump sum alimony can also be ordered in combination with other forms of alimony/property interest settlements: rehabilitative, permanent periodic, and special equities. Sort of a financial Chinese dinner. Lump sum alimony can be awarded by the court in an attempt to do what many judges believe a divorce should do—end the relationship between the parties once and for all. Instead of $200 per month forever, $100,000 now—or in a few large installments. It can be paid in installments and still not be periodic alimony and still not qualify as alimony for tax purposes.

Lump sum alimony has one real virtue to the spouse receiving it: Once ordered, it is a vested right not subject to modification or termination upon that spouse's remarriage.

The other version of lump sum alimony is one which got its best play in *Canakaris*. There the court said that lump sum alimony was one good way of providing for equitable distribution, for being fair to both partners in that economic venture called marriage, regardless of whose name the property, stock, bonds, boats, cars, etc., were in.

For example, suppose a marriage of twenty years, wife working outside the home very little or not at all, wife raising children, doing the traditional good wife bit; husband making professional advances and big bucks. House is in both their names. One car is in her name. All the other goodies are in his name. Divorce old style: she gets her car and half of the house—or even half of house and use of whole house until youngest child reaches eighteeen, and some periodic alimony.

Divorce new *Canakaris* style: she gets all she would have under old style plus some share—maybe half—of all the goodies he had stuck away in his name: the stocks, the bonds, the business, real estate.

Equitable Distribution

These are the magic words of alimony. Courts are still defining them, so only your lawyer can keep you up to date on what they mean for you. Should you wish to sound knowledgeable, remember the term that sprang onto the Florida legal scene back in 1980 in *Canakaris v. Canakaris*, a Supreme Court case in which the court spelled out specifically that a marriage was an economic partnership and that its breakup should not leave one partner out in the financial cold:

> A judge may award lump sum alimony to ensure an equitable distribution of property acquired during the marriage, provided the evidence reflects (1) a justification for

> such lump sum payment and, (2) financial ability of the other spouse to make such payment without substantially endangering his or her economic status.

Special Equity

This is a form of property settlement which beautifully demonstrates the value of having case law (judge made law) decide statute law. Once upon a time when our professed standards, if not our behavior, were stricter, the statute law said that wives who had committed adultery could not get alimony.

Faced with the prospect of scarlet-lettered but otherwise decent women struggling penniless after divorce, the courts found a way around this harsh law. The judges decided that any wife, with or without her scarlet letter, could be determined to have made a special contribution to the marriage above and beyond normal marital duties. Whenever that happened, they could say the wife had a special equity in property which entitled her to all or part of it upon divorce.

With the no-dollars-to-cheating-wives-law off the books, the special equity concept has stayed with us to protect the interest of a spouse's special contributions.

The term *special equity* is also used to cover a spouse's interest in property held in both names if the property or the funds for it came from sources outside the marriage. For example, rich aunt leaves $10,000 to husband who buys a certificate of deposit with it which he puts in both his name and his wife's. Unless it can be shown the certificate was meant as a gift to the wife, the husband has a good chance of claiming a special equity in the certificate and getting it all for himself.

It is difficult to generalize the present state of special equity law from the wide ranging facts of the cases which have reached the appellate courts. It is clear that in their attempts to be just, the judges have considered such factors as the length of the marriage, the source of the property, and the intention of the spouse who has the major claim to the property. Your lawyer can match your facts to the established cases.

The Marital Home

For many couples the marital home is their most valuable asset—if not the only asset. Therefore, what the court does with the home matters very much to husband, wife, and children. When there are children under eighteen, a court will often award the wife exclusive possession of the home till the last child turns eighteen. How the payments, insurance, taxes, and maintenance are paid for is worked out on a case by case basis depending on the parties' financial needs and abilities.

As is true of many matters in family law, much is in the hands of the trial judge.

> Although it is true that often, undoubtedly more often than not, exclusive possession of the marital home is awarded to the custodial parent of minor children, there is no rule of law mandating such an award. This decision also is one that lies soundly within the trial court's discretion. *Kuvin v. Kuvin*, 442 So.2d 203 (Fla. 1983)

The Two A's—Alimony and Adultery

An earlier section explained how the "special equity" came into being—to get around the old no-alimony-to-cheating-wives law.

The legislature, while backing down on no alimony to adulterous wives, retained its concern with the subject:

> Florida Statute 61.08 Alimony. The court may consider the adultery of a spouse and the circumstances thereof in determining

> whether alimony shall be awarded to such spouse and the amount of alimony, if any, to be awarded.

So you see that the scarlet letter is still important in the minds of the legislature and the judges, though the weight given to the subject is considerably less than it was years ago. The present language tells the trial judge, "You *may* consider the adultery of a spouse." It does not say "You *shall* consider the adultery of a spouse."

The truly significant language comes at the end of this section of Florida Statute 61.08:

> The court may consider any other factor necessary to do equity and justice between the parties.

Therefore, a judge doesn't have to say the adulterous spouse can't get alimony. In two well-known cases, the appeals courts have made this quite plain. In both *Smith v. Smith*, 378 So.2d 11 (Fla. 3d DCA 1979) and *Claughton v. Claughton*, 344 So.2d 944 (Fla. 3d DCA 1977) the appellate judges agreed that the incidents of adultery by the spouse seeking alimony were not the causes of the divorce nor were they related to the parties' financial situations.

When the court decides that the adultery was clearly the cause of the divorce, it is willing for the wife to make do with less alimony. *Martin v. Martin*, 366 So.2d 475 (Fla. 3d DCA 1979). If the husband's misconduct has reduced the marital resources, the court will consider this in the division of those resources so that the wife does not suffer from this action. *Williamson v. Williamson*, 367 So.2d 1016 (Fla. 1979).

More recent cases have dealt with other forms of marital misconduct and their relation to the amount and form of alimony. The misconduct has ranged from excessive drinking to shooting to being "a lifelong nag and intolerable companion." Your lawyer can tell you what relationship these cases have to yours. This is another reason for you to be completely honest with your attorney. He cannot protect you unless he knows the truth about your marriage.

For those of you who are a bit edgy on this subject, you may take comfort in *Linda v. Linda*, 352 So.2d 1208 (Fla. 4th DCA 1978) in which the appeal court held that, during discovery, the wife did not have to tell her lover's name. The adultery may matter; the name of the partner does not.

The Children

Custody—New Shape, New Name

Until July 1, 1982, child custody was, on the surface, a simple matter. Either the mother got the kids or—in fewer cases—the father did. The parent who didn't get custody got, usually, "reasonable visitation."

The parent with custody got all the decision-making duties about school, doctors, church attendance, sports participation, etc.

On July 1, 1982, all this changed. The following became the statute law of Florida:

> Florida Statute 63.13(2)
>
> 2. The court shall order that the parental responsibility for a minor child be shared by both parents unless the court finds that shared parental responsibility would be detrimental to the child. If the court determines that shared parental responsibility would be detrimental to the child, the court may order sole parental responsibility.

> a. "Shared parental responsibility" means that both parents retain full parental rights and responsibilities with respect to their child and requires both parents to confer so that major decisions affecting the welfare of the child will be determined jointly. In ordering shared parental responsibility, the court may consider the expressed desires of the parents and may grant to one party the ultimate responsibility over specific aspects of the child's welfare or may divide those aspects between the parties based on the best interests of the child. When it appears to the court to be in the best interests of the child, the court may order or the parties may agree how any such responsibility may include primary physical residence, education, medical and dental care, and any other responsibilities which the court finds unique to a particular family and/or in the best interests of the child.

Reactions to the law are strongly optimistic—and pessimistic. The optimists see the law preserving the value of family in spite of the dissolution of marriage; they see the children as benefiting from regular and frequent contact with both parents. The pessimists say if these people could agree and cooperate on anything—and especially a subject as emotion laden as their children—they would not be divorcing.

One significant change is the specific elimination of the "tender years doctrine." That doctrine was the legalistic way of saying "Little kids are better off with their mothers. Diapers, baby and all that." There were cases in which the "tender years" reached up to age seven or eight.

The Legislature's Dream World

One Florida Statute, 63.13(2) (b) (1), says, with an optimism apparently born of ignorance of the facts, "It is the public policy of this state to assure each minor child frequent and continuing contact with both parents." The fact is that between half and three-quarters of the divorced fathers fail to pay court-ordered child support and, of their own choice, have little or no contact with their children.

The Real World

Regardless of one's feelings about the wisdom of such public policy, the direction the Florida Legislature has given the courts is clear. "The court shall order that the parental responsibility for a minor child shall be shared by both parents . . . " The word *shall* is very important in this sentence, for the courts have held again and again that *shall* means *must* and does not have the element of option which *may* does. " . . . unless the court finds that shared parental responsibility would be detrimental to the child. If the court determines that shared parental responsibility would be detrimental to the child, the court may order sole parental responsibility."

Apparently, if you feel that you should be given sole responsibility for the children, then you and your lawyer must prove to the judge that letting your spouse share the responsibility would hurt the children. Without such proof the judge is required by law to order shared responsibility.

Sole parental responsibility, however, does not mean that the excluded spouse automatically has no right to visitation.

> Florida Statute 61.13 (2)(b)2. b.
> "Sole parental responsibility" means that responsibility for the minor child is given to one parent by the court, with or without rights of visitation to the other parent.

What happens to those parents who are not eager to be part of this social and legal experiment? What about those parents whose wishes fit the old way of divorce and custody? They may not be able to show harm if both parents have responsibility. They may not want to make such allegations and go to the expense of proving them. It would seem, then, that they can go along with the new form of parental responsibility, have the "primary physical residence" be with the mother, have the father pay some support and ignore the rest. If neither party goes back to court, the court is not going out looking for either one of them to check on how shared are the decisions about which doctor the child sees.

The New Tough Question

Florida Statute 61.13

(3) For purposes of shared parental responsibility and primary physical residence, the best interest of the child shall be determined by the court's consideration and evaluation of all factors affecting the best welfare and interests of the child, including, but not limited to:

a. The parent who is more likely to allow the child frequent and continuing contact with non-residential parent.

b. The love, affection, and other emotional ties existing between the parents and the child.

c. The capacity and disposition of the parents to provide the child with food, clothing, medical care or other remedial care recognized and permitted under the laws of this state in lieu of medical care, and other material need.

d. The length of time the child has lived in a stable, satisfactory environment and the desirability of maintaining continuity.

e. The permanence, as a family unit, of the existing or proposed custodial home.

f. The moral fitness of the parents.

g. The mental and physical health of the parents.

h. The home, school, and community record of the child.

i. The reasonable preference of the child, if the court deems the child to be of sufficient intelligence, understanding, and experience to express a preference.

j. Any other factor considered by the court to be relevant to a particular child custody dispute.

For those who want what this law offers—almost insists on—there may be a kicker in how the court decides primary physical residence. At least one circuit judge has commented that the first factor listed for the making of the primary physical residence is "The parent who is the more likely to allow the child frequent and continuing contact with the non-residential parent."

That judge contends that by placing first this standard for primary physical residence, the legislature intended that it be the most important standard. Thus, if this is true—or if judges believe it is true—parents contesting the issue of primary physical residence will be arguing "I will be better about your visitation with the child than you would be about my visitation." A little like one monk declaring to another: "But I am holier than thou."

While primary residence may be awarded to one parent, under the 1982 law, not all child-related decision-making goes with the award. Now both statute law and case law allow the court to place the child with one parent and yet follow the religious education wishes of the other parent. *Vazquez v. Vazquez*, 443 So.2d 313 (Fla. 4th DCA 1983). It would appear that the same principle would apply to medical, dental, or recreation decisions.

One real virtue to the shared parental responsibility law is that it allows for "face saving." A parent who doesn't want custody or who knows he isn't fit to have it can be half of a shared parental responsibility determination with the primary physical residence of the child going to the former spouse and with limited visitation. Still he can say he "shares" custody. This works even better for women who are under great social pressure and disdain if they don't have custody of their children. To the world at large, a mother without custody is a bad mother, unfit, tarnished before the law and her neighbors. This new law allows the mother without primary residence care of her child to say honestly that she shares custody.

Given this "sharing," a parent is more willing to agree to the other parent's having what used to be called custody. Thus, a nasty and expensive battle is avoided.

Regardless of which parent is named primary residential parent, the other parent under the new law has the right to see the child's important records.

> Florida Statute 61.13(2)(b)3.
> Access to records and information pertaining to a minor child, including but not limited to medical, dental, and school records, shall not be denied to a parent because such parent is not the child's primary residential parent.

At least one path to pettiness is cut off by the 1982 law.

Grandparents

The Legislature has been increasing the visitation rights which grandparents have. In 1982, the Legislature allowed grandparents to go to court to enforce rights which a parent got on their behalf. In 1984, the Legislature gave the grandparents themselves the right to petition the court for "reasonable rights of visitation." An adoption of a child by a stepparent does not terminate these visitation rights automatically. "However, the court may, after affording the grandparents an opportunity to be heard, determine that such termination of visitation rights is in the best interest of the child and rule accordingly." Florida Statute 61.1301.

Given the immaturity of some parents, a stable grandparent may be all a child can count on. The flip side, however, is that much dissension in the marriage and after can be blamed on interference by the spouses' parents.

Fault Revisited

When parents start fighting over whose home is

to be the primary residence of the children, or if one parent is to have sole responsibility, it is then that the question of *fault*, which was dropped with the creation of no-fault divorce, reappears.

It does not reappear with the name *fault* pinned to its jacket front. The label, instead, says, "The moral fitness of the parents." Bring out the allegations of alcohol and drug abuse, the kinky sex—anything.

What influence these allegations and the proof offered to support them will have depends on the particular judge who will be hearing them. As was pointed out in the definition of *judge*, much depends on the individual judge's background and philosophy. Florida, ranging from rural to urban and back again within less than a hundred miles, has some widely differing opinions on this matter. Some judges see anything a parent does as having an effect on the child. Others hold that it is the concern of the court only as to what is done in the presence of the child. Without drawing pictures, one can see how this divergence of viewpoints can produce quite different decisions depending on who is the judge.

Who Goes Where?

Shared parental responsibility has been the law in Florida for so short a time, there is little case law to tell the public what it means, how it is to be put into practice. As the advertising people would say: "Watch this space." This complicated and emotion-laden area is sure to generate many appellate cases.

There are various ways children can be divided up between parents. The most common is that in which, no matter what name is given to the arrangement, the child or children live most of the time with one parent and have visitation with the other parent. Visitation can be as often as every weekend and every Wednesday night, or it can be one week during Christmas vacation and two weeks in the summer.

Another way is what is called rotating custody. Custody is a word which dies hard, as it has such clear meaning to most people. The child lives six months (or some other unit of time) with one parent and six with the other. This tends to get court approval only if both parents live in the same school district, and if this method doesn't create more problems than it solves.

How all this is seen by at least one child is reported by Naomi Hample in her charming study of children and their families, *Hugging, Hitting and Other Family Matters*. Linda, with her own spelling, wrote:

> My family is almost never together. My parents are separated. My Mother is with us from Wendsday to Saturday and my father from Sunday to Wendsday. I don't know how they made the schedule which I'm not very crazy about but I know they both love me which is terrific.

Split custody (or primary physical residence) is another way of handling a family's break-up. One or more children go to one parent; the other(s) to the other parent. On the surface, there is something repulsive about this. It smacks of treating the children as property. One parent gets the Dodge, the other the Chevrolet. And in some cases, that element may be the dominant one. However, skipping Freud, etc., the parents and the court may recognize that, for whatever reasons, some children in a family are better off with one parent, while the other children are better off with the other parent.

Case law runs rather strongly against split custody: *Scott v. Scott*, 401 So.2d 879 (1981); *Collier v. Collier*, 384 So.2d 697 (1980); and *Bienvenue v. Bienvenue*, 380 So.2d 1164 (3rd DCA 1980).

A highly informal survey of judges reveals wide ranging opinions on split custody. One stuck to the official party line of the cases: it must be clearly shown to be in the best interest of the child. One judge was firm in declaring: "If ever the children need to be together it is now, when their family is dividing." Another, recognizing that splits are not only between parents, said that during a time of family reorganization, the children could reasonably and with no harm go to the parent with whom they are most comfortable.

Spouse Abuse

With one exception, the Legislature leaves up to the court the question of what it would take to make shared parental responsibility detrimental to the child. The 1984 Legislature added one specific condition to the law: "The court shall consider evidence of spouse abuse as evidence of detriment to the child." Not proof—evidence.

The law goes on to say, "If the court finds that spouse abuse has occurred between the parties, the court may award sole parental responsibility to the abused spouse, and make such arrangements for visitation as will best protect the child and the abused spouse from further harm." Note that the law says *may*, not *shall*. Yet, please also note the firm concern of the law with protection of the child and the abused spouse. The Legislature clearly supports the research revealing that children suffer from great fear if a parent is hurt even if the child himself is never touched. Although only the spouse is abused, the child also must be protected from "further" harm.

How is a Custody Decision Made?

What will affect a judge's thinking on which parent should have sole parental responsibility or the primary residence under shared parental responsibility? From a study of the case law and from listening to thoughtful judges speak at legal meetings, I find that the following appear to be highly important:

1. The concept of fault in the marriage break-up insofar as it applies to one's moral fitness as a parent. The basic question judges seem to ask: What impact will this behavior have on the child?

2. The facts and opinions of those outside the family who have been in a good position to observe the parent's relationship with the child. The jargon term is "parenting skills." Here, the schoolteacher may be highly valuable if she can report parent involvement with homework and school projects. A neighbor who has seen and heard the parent dealing with the child can be

> useful, especially if he or she has visited in the home on a frequent and casual basis. A counselor, from either the school or outside, can be effective if he or she doesn't have a reputation for being a mental health hired gun.

The courts are more and more reliant on the same professionals that the family would have used had there been no divorce. This use of non-state action rather than state action (the courts) reduces the state's intrusion into the private lives of the citizens, areas which are not legal areas.

There is one easy and often highly effective way to put all these people together for the judge before the hearing ever starts. In fact, with luck, this way is so effective at organizing objective information that the parties may reach an agreement without a hearing/fight.

> Florida Statute 61.20. Social investigation and recommendations when child custody is in issue. In any action where the custody of a minor child is in issue, the court may request the Department of Health and Rehabilitative Services or qualified staff of the court to make an investigation and social study concerning all pertinent details relating to the child and each parent. The department or qualified staff of the court shall furnish the court with a written report with its recommendation with a written statement of facts found in its social investiga-

> tions on which its recommendations are based. The court may consider the information contained in the report in making a decision on the child's custody and the technical rules of evidence do not exclude such report from consideration.

Either party may ask the court to order such a study, or the court may, on its own, decide to order one. It is my experience that the courts welcome the help in making a difficult decision which is not in the judge's field of training. The husband and wife have a chance to read the results of the study before the hearing and may, at the hearing, challenge the alleged facts in the report, its conclusions or both.

Child Support

Child support is based on the child's needs and the parents' ability to pay. For low and low-middle income families, there really is no analysis of the child's need, for the parents' paying ability is such that the child's needs—above the very basic—just don't matter. Neither blood nor child support can come from a turnip.

It is with the middle, upper-middle, and upper economic classes that child support becomes a legal and emotional battleground. How many lessons and camps does a child need? Sometimes, it appears that the answer is "as many as there is money to pay for."

At least one circuit judge has recently tried to recognize a certain basic reality regarding child support: Children grow, they do not shrink. As they grow, they eat more, their clothes cost more, and they have more activities that require funds. His recognition took the form of a support order in which the father was to pay $300 a month until the child was five; $400 per month until the child was ten; and $500 per month thereafter.

The appellate court said, "No go." More exactly, it said, "Judgments providing for automatic changes in support payments are generally disfavored, as there is no evidentiary basis for the determination of future events, for there exists an adequate procedure for modification when changes in the circumstances of the parties do occur." *Penkoski v. Patterson*, 440 So.2d 45 (Fla. 1st DCA 1983.

The court ignores the certainty of a child's growth as a future event. And the Court places the burden of modification on the parent with the child—usually the mother, who is usually the one less well equipped to hire a lawyer for a modification order granting an increase.

Appellate Judge James Joanos, writing the dissent, perceptively noted:

> To discourage the entry of forward looking judgments and to encourage the frequent return to the courtroom should not be favored. The " . . . adequate procedure for modification . . . " referred to by the majority is both expensive and fraught with emotional shock. It oftentimes continues a war that should have ended long before. It is also a drain upon the labors of the trial bench.

One can only hope the dissent will, before long, become the majority.

Support Versus Visitation

Unlike "Love and Marriage," one can have one without the other. When the parent who has the day-to-day care of the child is not getting the child support ordered by the court, she cannot retaliate by denying visitation to her former spouse. No matter how angry she is about the lack of support, she cannot say, "No money, no visit."

And, in turn, a father whose former wife refuses to let him see the child, cannot say "No visit, no money." Each angry parent must, instead, return to the court for it to order the payment of support and the visitation.

It is worth remembering the theory backing the above: that these rights—support and visitation—belong to the child, not the parents. In legalese, these rights "vest" in the child.

Modification

Initial decisions about primary physical residence and the amount of child support are not forever. All are subject to modification if there has occurred a "substantial and material change in the circumstances of the parties." At this point the children are among the parties. For a residence change to be ordered, the parent urging the change must also show that the change would be in the best interest of the child, that not to make the change would be to the child's detriment. This double requirement is what lawyers and judges like to call a two pronged test:

1. A material and substantial change in circumstances.
2. The best interests of the child.

Now, what constitutes a material and substantial change and the best interest of the child are matters for the judge to decide.

In custody matters, it is easier to say what it is not than what it is. It is not what the children want, though that is a consideration. It is not that one parent has remarried, thus creating a "whole home." It is not, barring more, that the parent with whom the child lives has a live-in lover. It can well be a combination of all these factors.

Child support, too, can be modified. Such modification requires proof of a material and substantial change in circumstances. As support is geared to a balance of the child's need and the parent's ability to pay, modification cannot be made almost automatically in response to those remarkable facts of nature and economics: children grow and, as larger beings, cost more to feed and clothe.

One has to prove that something other than that has taken place. Judges seem to consider inflation a suitable peg on which to hang increased support. *Peterson v. Peterson*, 392 So.2d 298 (Fla. 4th DCA 1981), *Davis v. Fisher*, 391 So.2d 810 (Fla. 5th DCA 1980) rev. dism. 397 So.2d 777, *Pope v. Pope*, 342 So.2d 1000 (Fla. 4th DCA 1977). And, of course, any real change in the financial conditions of the parents may justify a change. Children can be expected to share in the good fortune of the parents. Hit it lucky in some out-of-state lottery and expect to share with your children. The reverse applies, too. The support-paying father who falls seriously ill will not be expected to meet the payments he did before the illness.

The 1982 shared parental responsibility law is not a basis for modification; so those who were divorced and had their custody/visitation conditions set before July 1982, have no claim on the court's time if that is all they can say has changed. *Iljazi v. Iljazi*, 326 So.2d 326 (Fla. 2d DCA 1983). The change was not in the parties, but in the law.

The Collection of Alimony and Child Support

The 1984 Florida Legislature made drastic changes in the alimony and child support collection laws. The new laws require that court ordered alimony and child support be paid to a central office within each county or judicial circuit. That office, in turn, pays the alimony/support to the ex-wife. Should these payments become thirty days past due, they are considered delinquent. The central office, after giving the ex-spouse a fifteen day notice, will then serve an income deduction order on the ex-spouse's employer. The employer must deduct the amount ordered and send it to the central office for forwarding to the support-receiving spouse.

The law allows the judge to make a specific exception in his order and not have the alimony/support go to the central office. However, should either ex-spouse later wish, application to the central office can be made and all payments thereafter must go through the central office. The ex-spouse doesn't have to go to court again for this change to be made.

Parental Conduct

Whether it is shared parental responsibility or custody with visitation, there will be many, many times when former spouses will have to meet for the exchanging of children—weekends, holidays. The possibilities for conflict are almost unlimited. What is intended to hurt a former spouse, of course, hurts the child.

Judith Martin, writing as Miss Manners, goes right to the heart of the matter. "Anyone mature enough to get divorced ought to be able to behave; anyone regularly possessed by uncontrollable feelings ought not to have custody of small children." After reviewing the basic "rules" of child exchange—being on time, having clothes and toys ready—she sums up: "It is the cheerful, happy cooperative parent who both wins the heart of the child, and rubs it into the former spouse just how happy living without that person can be."

The Future

If you divorce and have no children and were not intertwined with your spouse's business, your future, at least on the surface, may be as if you never married and divorced. Society and the law, for the most part, give you a clean slate. Women can have their maiden names restored; rings can be returned, sold or just shoved to the back of the drawer. Any twinge of regret or sadness can be absolutely private or shared with a therapist.

Those of you with children, however, face quite a different range of choices. You will be living with, or visiting, constant reminders of your marriage and divorce. The financial circumstances, either actual or spouse contrived, may govern a large portion of your life. Your former spouse's behavior will affect not just you but your children. With your children, either in the background or foreground, you will continue to deal with those aspects of your former spouse which contributed to the breaking of the marriage. Too, you may have to confront new behaviors which have developed to punish you for the divorce/alimony/child support.

Very few of the formerly married with children report good relations with former spouses. Many just cope and endure. Others return to court. There appears to be one almost certain reaction in the world of divorce and custody. When one former spouse remarries, that remarriage triggers some form of illogical, unusual behavior on the part of the non-marrying spouse. This holds true even if the non-marrying spouse was the one who wanted the divorce, the one who thought the former spouse a sexless, dull blob.

This is when the lawyers can count on the phone ringing with charges ranging from support arrearages to visitation violations. In drastic cases, an otherwise calm parent will snatch a child. When a former client is upset, the lawyer should be available to help. This is also the time for the lawyer to strive for calm, to remember the unwritten but real obligation he has to the Court and to the child—to counsel the client-parent about the best interests of the child.

Such emotional flurries can lead to thousands of dollars in legal fees and little or no improvement in the welfare of either parent or child. A lot of hurtful words will have been said and heard and a lot of money will have changed hands, but little good will come of the charges and counter charges.

If your former spouse is remarrying or you are, beware the last attack of jealousy. Don't waste your energy on this. Save your energy for what may be worse problems ahead: step-children. In past decades children usually went with the mother after the divorce. So, if a divorced mother married some divorced father she brought all her children and he brought none of his. She was the "real" mother to all, he was step-father to all. Each child ended up with the same "real" brothers and sisters as before.

But in future decades, as joint custody replaces sole custody, divorced mothers with one or more part-time children will marry fathers with one or more part-time children. In the resulting home each of the adults will be a "real" parent to some of the children but a step-parent to others; all of the children are stepchildren to one or other of the parents, and all have a "real" parent who lives somewhere else. Some of the brothers and sisters aren't "real" brothers and sisters, "even though I have to share my things with them." Everybody—adult and child alike—has a dual role in this home. And to complicate matters still further, each belongs in some way to another home somewhere else.

And as if these child-parent relations weren't complex enough already, some of these parents will now add more children. The possible combinations and permutations for trouble quickly become astronomical—far worse than they were for the first marriage—and that failed. Armed with nothing more than a rosy glow, and having seen *With Six You Get*

Egg Roll too many times, parents marry again and create new families which turn out to be entirely unlike *The Brady Bunch*.

Ann Landers has observed repeatedly, "Nine times out of ten, when second marriages fail, it is because of the children from a previous marriage. Invariably, the spouse sides with his (or her) kids and the marriage goes down the drain."

With luck, the problems will not be legal. You will not need a lawyer. But you should give serious thought to working with a family counselor or at least studying one of the several good books on the subject.

Not to Worry—Forewarned is Forearmed—and Other Cliches

We jaundiced-eyed cynics hate to admit it, but there is much good in the world, much happiness. This good, this happiness, flows to those who use their intelligence with care, who learn the rules and either follow them or change them, and who are kind to others and themselves. Good luck!

APPENDIX

The following forms and the sample dissolution of marriage petition may give you a better understanding of the explanations in the main parts of this book. The recommended reading should also help, especially if you don't see a counselor.

A Simple Sample Petition For a Dissolution of Marriage

IN THE CIRCUIT COURT OF THE
SECOND JUDICIAL CIRCUIT, IN
AND FOR LEON COUNTY, FLORIDA

CASE NO.

IN RE: The Marriage of
MARY A. SAMPLE,
Wife/Petitioner,
and
JOHN B. SAMPLE,
Husband/Respondent.

____/

PETITION FOR DISSOLUTION OF MARRIAGE

COMES NOW the Petitioner, Mary A. Sample, by and through her undersigned attorney, and alleges:

1. This is an action for dissolution of marriage between Petitioner, Mary A. Sample, and Respondent, John B. Sample.
2. Petitioner has been a resident of Florida for more than six months before filing this petition.
3. Petitioner and Respondent were married to each other on February 14, 1979, in Venice, Florida, and cohabitated together as husband and wife until October, 1984.
4. Neither party is a member of the armed forces of the United States of America on active duty.
5. One child was born of the marriage of the parties, John B. Sample, Jr., age 4, born January 1, 1980. No other children are anticipated.
6. Petitioner is a fit and proper person to provide the minor child's primary residence, and it is in the best interest of the child that his primary residence be with his mother, the Petitioner.
7. Petitioner requires and Respondent is well able to provide $300.00 a month in financial support for the minor child, and provide medical and dental insurance for the child.
8. Petitioner claims a special equity in the household furnishings in that she has made all the payments on them from her separate funds.
9. There are debts of the parties to each other and to third parties that need to be equitably divided by this court.
10. Petitioner has been required to retain the undersigned to represent her in this action, but is unable to pay for such legal services. Respondent is well able to pay Petitioner's attorney's fees and the costs of this action.

11. The marriage of the parties is irretrievably broken.

WHEREFORE, Petitioner prays that this Court will:

1. Dissolve the marriage between the parties.

2. Order that the minor child's primary residency shall be with the mother, subject to reasonable visitation of the Respondent.

3. Require the Respondent to pay $300 per month support for the child and to maintain medical and dental insurance policies for the benefit of the child.

4. Award the household furnishings to the Petitioner.

5. Equitably divide the financial obligations which the parties have to each other and to third parties.

6. Require the Respondent to pay the Petitioner's attorney's fee and costs of this action.

____

Divorce Lawyer
100 Courthouse Way
Tallahassee, FL 32300
(904) 000-0000

STATE OF FLORIDA
COUNTY OF LEON

BEFORE ME, the undersigned authority, on this day personally appeared MARY A. SAMPLE, who, first being duly sworn, deposes and says that she is the Petitioner named in the above and foregoing Petition for Dissolution of Marriage; that she has read the same, knows the contents thereof, and that the same is true and correct to the best of her knowledge and belief.

____

MARY A. SAMPLE

SWORN AND SUBSCRIBED to before me this____day of October, 1984 in the State and County aforementioned.

____

NOTARY PUBLIC

My commission expires:

Affidavit for Custody of Children

STATE OF FLORIDA
COUNTY OF LEON

BEFORE ME, the undersigned authority, personally appeared the affiant, who is a party in the dissolution of marriage or custody proceeding in which this affidavit is filed, and upon being duly sworn deposes and says:

1. That the child involved in this proceeding and its age and present address are as follows: John B. Sample, Jr., four years, 1660 King Charles Road, Tallahassee, Florida.
2. That the places where the child has lived within the last five years are as follows:

From birth to January, 1983
410 Portia Drive
Venice, Florida
From January, 1983, to the present
1660 King Charles Road
Tallahassee, Florida

3. The names and present addresses of the persons with whom the child has lived during the last five years are as follows: Mary A. Sample, 1660 King Charles Road, Tallahassee, Florida; John B. Sample, 515 Prosser Way, Tallahassee, Florida; Martha S. Acheson, 410 Portia Drive, Venice, Florida.
4. The affiant has not participated as a party or as a witness or in any other capacity in any other litigation concerning the custody of the same child in this or any other state.

5. The affiant does not have information of any custody proceeding concerning the child pending in a court of this or any other state.

6. The affiant does not know of any person not a party to proceedings who has physical custody of the child or claims to have custody or physical rights with respect to the child.

____

MARY A. SAMPLE

Sworn to and subscribed before me this____day of ____________, 1984.

____

NOTARY PUBLIC

My commission expires:

Worksheet for Preparing a Financial Affidavit

If you are a party in a divorce action, you are required by the Florida Rules of Civil Procedure to file with the court a financial affidavit showing your income and expenses, your assets and liabilities.

The worksheet which follows will help you by reminding you of a great number of items you don't want to overlook. In listing income and expenses be sure to indicate whether a particular amount is for each week, each month, or each year.

If you have no records of your actual expenses for recreation, incidentals, and such items, just put down your best estimate.

For each asset and liability, you will need to indicate who is the owner. You might use these abbreviations: H for husband, W for wife, J/W for owned jointly with wife, J/H for jointly with husband, J/O for jointly with other. Where you own a partial interest, tell the total value and indicate what fraction is yours.

Giving a fully accurate and truthful report will serve you best.

WORKSHEET FOR FINANCIAL AFFIDAVIT

Occupation: ____________________

Employed By: ____________________

Pay Period: ____________________

Next Pay Day: ____________________

Rate of Pay: $ ____________________ (week, month, year)

INCOME:	Week	Month	Year
Average GROSS wage	______	______	______
Less Deductions:			
Federal Income Tax	______	______	______
Social Security	______	______	______
Other	______	______	______
Total Deductions	______	______	______
Average NET Wage	______	______	______
Itemized Other Income			
__________________	______	______	______
__________________	______	______	______
TOTAL NET INCOME	______	______	______
EXPENSES:			
Rent	______	______	______
House Payments	______	______	______
Taxes (on home)	______	______	______
Taxes (on other realty)	______	______	______
Taxes (on personal property)	______	______	______
Food (for___members)	______	______	______
Milk	______	______	______
Special Diet	______	______	______
School Lunches	______	______	______
Kindergarten/Nursery Costs	______	______	______
Maid	______	______	______
Babysitter	______	______	______
School Supplies	______	______	______
Tuition	______	______	______

EXPENSES: (continued)	Week	Month	Year
School Transportation	______	______	______
Dancing/Music Lessons	______	______	______
Other School Expenses (tutoring, club dues)	______	______	______
Clothing (self)	______	______	______
Clothing (children)	______	______	______
Laundry/Dry Cleaning	______	______	______
Doctor	______	______	______
Dentist/Orthodontist	______	______	______
Optician	______	______	______
Hospital	______	______	______
Drugs, Vitamins, etc.	______	______	______
Other Medical Expenses	______	______	______
Transportation (bus, taxi, car pool)	______	______	______
Car Payment (rent__, own__)	______	______	______
Gas, Oil, Repairs	______	______	______
Tag, Driver's License, etc.	______	______	______
Telephone	______	______	______
Electricity	______	______	______
Natural Gas	______	______	______
Heating Fuel	______	______	______
Water	______	______	______
Sewer Charge	______	______	______
Garbage Collection	______	______	______
Other Utility Charges	______	______	______
Insurance:	______	______	______
House	______	______	______
Car (____no. of cars)	______	______	______

EXPENSES: (continued)	Week	Month	Year
Health			
(individual____family____)	____	____	____
Disability	____	____	____
Life (insured:____________)	____	____	____
Life (insured:____________)	____	____	____
Life (insured:____________)	____	____	____
Newspaper	____	____	____
Magazines and Books	____	____	____
Dues (clubs, union, etc.)	____	____	____
Contributions-Charity	____	____	____
Contributions-Church	____	____	____
Home repairs and yard work	____	____	____
Beauty Salon	____	____	____
Hair Cuts	____	____	____
Recreation:	____	____	____
Self	____	____	____
Children	____	____	____
Incidentals	____	____	____
____________	____	____	____
____________	____	____	____
Payments on Bills:			
____________	____	____	____
____________	____	____	____
____________	____	____	____
____________	____	____	____
____________	____	____	____
____________	____	____	____
TOTAL EXPENSES	____	____	____

SUMMARY	____	____	____
Net Income	____	____	____
Less Expenses	____	____	____
NET	____	____	____

ASSETS as of (date)________

Checking Accounts:

Bank Name	Account No.	Owner	Amount

Savings Accounts or Certificates of Deposit:

Bank Name	Account No.	Owner	Amount (and Date of C.D. Maturity)

Stocks and Bonds:

Name	Owner	Date of Purchase	Cost	Market Value

Real Estate:

Description (address)	Owner	Cost	Mortgage Amount	Market Value

Automobiles:

Make/Model	Title Owner	Driver	Lien Payments	Market Value

Boats, Airplanes, Other Vehicles:

Description	Title Owner	Lien Payments	Market Value

Life Insurance:

Insured	Name of Company	Amount	Cash Value

Other Assets (over $500):

Description	Location	Value

LIABILITIES:

Real Estate Mortgages:

Description	Amount	Payment

Credit Union Debts:

Name	Amount	Payment

Bank Loans:

Name	Purpose of Loan	Amount	Payment

Auto Loans:

Description	Lender	Person Liable	Amount	Payment

Other Notes, Loans, Charge Accounts:

Lender	Person Liable	Amount	Payment
______	______	______	______
______	______	______	______

Liability for Taxes: $______

SUMMARY:
TOTAL ASSETS $______
TOTAL LIABILITIES ______
NET WORTH: $______

Financial Affadavit

IN THE CIRCUIT COURT OF THE
SECOND JUDICIAL CIRCUIT, IN
AND FOR   COUNTY, FLORIDA

CASE NO.

IN RE: The Marriage of

and

____________________________/

FINANCIAL AFFIDAVIT

STATE OF FLORIDA
COUNTY OF

BEFORE ME, the undersigned authority, personally appeared _______________, who was sworn and says that the following statement of Affiant's employment, income, expenses, assets, and liabilities is true:

Occupation: ____

Employed By: ____

Business Address: ______________________________________

Pay Period: __________________ Next Pay Day: _____________

Rate of Pay: ______________________ Per: ___________________

ITEM I: INCOME

Average GROSS wage per month .... $__________

Less Deductions:

Federal Income Tax .... $__________

Social Security .... $__________

Other (Itemized) __________

____

____

TOTAL DEDUCTIONS .... $__________

Average NET wage per month .... $__________

OTHER INCOME (Itemized: include child support and alimony)

______________________________________ $__________

______________________________________ $__________

______________________________________ $__________

TOTAL NET INCOME PER MONTH ..... $__________

ITEM 2: EXPENSES (Averaged on a monthly basis):

How many persons are included? __________

Rent, house payments .... $__________

Food .... $__________

Clothing .... $__________

Incidentals .... $__________

Medical & Dental .... $__________

Transportation: $__________

Gas .... $__________

Insurance .... $__________

Car Payment .... $__________

Recreation .... $__________

Cable TV .... $__________

Insurance:
  **Health & Hospitalization .... $________
  **Life .... $________
  *Homeowners .... $________
*Taxes (Property) .... $________
(*Do not list here if included in house payment)
(**Do not list here if included in a payroll deduction plan)
Utilities:
  Electricity .... $________
  Gas .... $________
  Telephone .... $________
  Waste Disposal .... $________
Child support paid .... $________
Alimony paid .... $________
Payment on bills: (Itemized: include credit cards and charge accounts)

________________________________ $________
________________________________ $________
________________________________ $________
________________________________ $________
________________________________ $________

TOTAL EXPENSES .... $________

SUMMARY: Net Income .... $________
Less Expenses .... $________
TOTAL .... $________

ITEM 3: ASSETS

Cash on hand or in banks .... $________

Stocks, bonds, notes, etc. .... $________

Automobiles .... $________

Real Estate:

Home .... $________

Other Real Property (Itemize)

____________________ $________

____________________ $________

____________________ $________

Personal Property (Include clothing, furniture, jewelry, art work, etc.) .... $________

Other assets: (Include boats, airplanes, campers, copyrights, patents, antiques, collections, etc., and itemize)

____________________ $________

____________________ $________

____________________ $________

TOTAL ASSETS .... $________

ITEM 4: LIABILITIES

Credit Union . . . . $__________

Real Estate Mortgages . . . . $__________

Automobile Loans . . . . $__________

Other notes, debts & loans (Itemize: include charge accounts & credit cards)

______________________________________ $__________

______________________________________ $__________

______________________________________ $__________

______________________________________ $__________

TOTAL LIABILITIES . . . . $__________

____

Affiant

Sworn to and subscribed before me on this_____day of________________,1984.

____

NOTARY PUBLIC

Recommended Reading

Galper, Mariam. *Co-Parenting, Sharing Your Child Equally.* Philadelphia: Running Press, 1978.

Hample, Naomi, and Hample, Stuart. *Hugging, Hitting and Other Family Matters.* New York: The Dial Press, 1979.

Krantzler, Mel. *Creative Divorce.* New York: New American Library, 1974.

Salk, Lee. *What Every Child Would Like Parents to Know About Divorce.* New York: Warner, 1979.

Triere, Lynette. *Learning to Leave.* Chicago: Contemporary Books, Inc., 1982.